The Local SEO Handbook

Learn the basics of local SEO to impact your marketing by using the R.A.P.

By: Jonathan Alonso

Jonathan Alonso

Copyright © 2018 Jonathan Alonso

All rights reserved.

ISBN: 9781720029076

There is no secret formula for digital marketing. it takes hard work, experimenting, and learning from your peers. Never believe someone who claims to be an "expert" or offers a "proprietary" system. there is no secret sauce in marketing, we all learn from each other.

Jonathan Alonso

CONTENTS

	Acknowledgments	i
1	How it all Began	8
2	The Moments that Matter	10
3	How do we start?	12
4	The Customer Journey	16
5	Understand Micro-Moments	19
6	Roll up Our Sleeves	24
7	What is R.A.P	31
8	Let's Be Relevant	32
9	Build Authority	41
10	Proximity & Trust	47
11	Reviews	50
12	Managing Multiple Locations	55
13	Social Features	57
	Resources	59

The Local SEO Handbook

ACKNOWLEDGMENTS

Thank you,

First, thank you to my Lord and Savior, Jesus Christ, because He inspires me every day.

To my beautiful wife and best friend Kristy, thank you for the idea to put my knowledge on paper, and to my family and friends for always being positive about my ideas, I say a big thank you.

Follow me on social

Instagram: @jongeek
LinkedIn: alonsojon
Facebook: jongeekmarketing
Twitter @jongeek

Introduction

Running a business can be difficult nowadays because there is competition everywhere and your competitors are always trying to find the edge over you. There has to be a way to impact your sales with a slim budget, right? And there has to be an easier way to capture local customers when they really need or want you, correct? That's where digital marketing plays a vital role in any business.

In the past, people relied on word-of-mouth recommendations and questions in their time of need for a service or product, which took a lot more time and the information might have been unreliable. Now we can get our answers in seconds and we have the opportunity to view the quality of service with recommendations that we call "reviews". Our generation has the power of answers and information in the palm of their hands.

Knowing how to embed your business in time that your potential customers need you is the key to winning in today's business world. This local SEO strategy can help you get your business where it is found and trusted.

Chapter 1
How it all Began

During my start at one of my recent projects at a large tech repair franchise, one thing was clear; there is a moment of emergency when you need a product or service like breaking a phone. As I further studied this, I noticed that most of the keywords that people were using to find the company I was working for involved "near me" or terms that included geography like "Atlanta," "Miami," or "Chicago" and other city specific attributions.

Other than the current investments in paid advertisement we saw a need that was bigger than just investments in paid ads and the constant optimization of organic rankings. Our findings showed that 70% of consumers were focused on Google Maps before they even interacted with our site, and data from Google themselves corroborated this. In addition, there is the fact that 76% of people that visit a Google listing also visit the retail location within that same day, with 28% of those same users ending up in a purchase.

These are staggering numbers, but I realized that it's the direct correlation of how Google is looking to personalize their search. Personalization of search means the ability to serve you search engine results based on your location, time, needs and past searches. It creates an ability for you to get the most convenient results based on how Google has analyzed your data. As I looked at this I understood the amazing opportunity that Local SEO could render to this company.

I walked in into the owner's office on a one to one meeting we had scheduled, and I explained the journey of a how a customer would come to find us via Google Maps with our data to prove our current traffic. I peaked his interest as he is also a fellow data geek; however, one question remained during my presentation that the owner made me aware of.

He asked: "How does local ranking work? How can we explain this to our franchisees?"

Great question, even though I knew how to do it, I had never broken it down. As an analyst, I have always just done the work or worked with vendors and vetted those vendors based on my past success. I really knew that this was part of the success and needed to find solutions that could help us succeed and scale our local SEO strategy.

Chapter 2
The Moments that Matter

As I went home that evening, I pondered what the correct next steps to taking on such a tremendous project were. At the moment, the organization I was doing work for was at around 200 locations, in which, including an aggressive growth of 50% more by 2018, I had to get working on a system that would work as soon as possible, and that would be able to scale with the franchise. I also wanted to deliver quality research that would impact their franchisees to discover the power of local SEO and how it would impact their bottom line.

One of my primary resources for marketing is the marketing blog ThinkwithGoogle.com, and they lay out data points, studies, experiments, and case studies. This is how I have approached a lot of my strategies in many industries I have worked with, and they also have some excellent stats for presentations.

As I read many of the current Local SEO guides and Google's recommendations one of the biggest studies that stood out to me is one that Google did a few years ago called "Micro-Moments"

Micro-moments is defined by "moments" that occur when someone reacts and turns to any type of device to want to learn, research, discover, buy, and find or watch something. These are called "Moments," and moments are defined as "intent-rich" decisions.

I have known this all along but taking the current customer journey of my project, I imagined these customers pulling out their mobile phone at the moment that they saw their computer drop in the pool. According to Google, 40% of searches that had "intent" came from a cell phone, and this has been a significant shift in the last few years. Google has put a lot of resources into studying the impact of phones versus desktop, and phones have taken over.

Some of these studies have led into Google redefining their web search experience, the design on mobile devices and even to its most currently deployed advancement in Google seeing mobile traffic as more important than the desktop with their shift to mobile-first indexing.

This is how some of my information gatherings started—analyzing the rise of immediate need searches that could impact local business.

Using this study, we can assume that there is now a need for your business to be within those searches right?

Now think about the following:

Imagine the impact of being relevant to these searches when someone needs your services or products
The number of searches in your local area that you may be missing out on
Reflect on what your current customers do to find you, and how much more powerful this would be online

Tip: Understand more about Micro-moments
I will be covering more about this in later chapters, I recommend watching this commercial Google created to help people understand how this strategy could fit into your business:
https://youtu.be/mNltt5_LbG8

Chapter 3
How do we start?

Google's Mission statement is: "To organize the world's information and make it universally accessible and useful."

Just think of that statement for a second. To understand how this impacts your business, you would have to structure your mindset to consider the following:

1. How can my business be relevant, impactful and informational for search engine customers? (Yes, if you search on Google you are their customer)

2. What can my business offer to my customers that my competitors are not offering on Google?

3. What values do I stand for that can make an impact for good online?

4. What questions do my customers have that I can answer for them?

One thing to keep in mind is that when a person searches on any search engine, there are three ways your customers can find you—they can find you on Paid ads, Directory Listings, and Organic search results.

The Anatomy of Search

Picture This: You're looking for a restaurant to eat near your office, then you will head to your office computer or your cell phone and search for what you're in the mood for, right? You quickly head to Google.com and type the following in the search bar: "Restaurant near me" or "sushi near me." Your search will bring a few links on the top of search results that display "ad" on top, after, you should also see three listings that display a map with restaurant names and a call or directions button, and under the maps, you will notice blue colored listings.

Blended Searches

All of this information grouped together is what we call "Blended Search"; they are a blend of all types of information in one search, not just website results. Blended searches include data like news, images, videos or even books making your search experience richer and personal.

Personal Search

Yes, Google went personal, In almost every search you see, you will start noticing relevant information that Google can show you that informs you on searches that are "dedicated to you." We call this "Personal search." because the data it shows is based on your consumption of data, websites you've visited, your location and proximity to the businesses around you, and in some cases who you are, calendar updates, your favorites and more.

This is important to know for your business because it helps you understand the opportunities that you can go after to create an impact. Knowing this can allow your business to generate valuable data about your products or services in the form of videos, meaningful images, and what we call featured snippets.

So let's break down your current search for "Restaurants near me."

Paid Ads

Paid ads are also known as "Paid Search" and play a part in your investment in attracting customers to keywords you want to show up for, and you pay when a person clicks on your ad and goes to your website (this is called PPC, Pay-Per-Click).

These ads show up at the beginning of a search and sometimes in the bottom of search results in desktop and mobile and will be identified with a small box that says "ad." You pay to be in those positions; for example, if you want to show up for customers looking for a plumber at 2 am that might need an immediate fix, then using some research and tools you may identify that the right keyword will be "24-hour plumber" or "plumber near me open now."

The process is simplified above, but it is complicated. Many ad agencies have departments dedicated to doing this for you, but Google has tools to teach small business how to do this themselves as well. The platform Google uses is called Google Ads, Formerly Google Adwords.

Bing also has its alternative to Google Adwords, and it is called Bing Ads. The cool feature Bing includes is that you can just copy your campaigns from your Google Adwords account over to Bing and it will make an exact carbon copy so that you can expand your marketing to the 2 top major search engines.

You will then notice the three directory listings shown below the ads....

Google Maps / Local Directory *(this is where we do Local SEO)*.

This is where we are focusing the book on. The idea of Google maps started in Feb 2005 and was originally invented by two Danish brothers, Lars and Jens Eilstrup Rasmussen (their project was acquired by Google and later named "Google Maps").

Let's go back a few paragraphs, do you remember Google's mission to make "information accessible"? This is part of it, by helping people find directions, locations and navigating them was a cutting-edge idea, and now it is one of the most used applications and web apps in the world.

Now put yourself in an advertiser's mindset, what can this mean for your business? Imagine keeping your business information up to date and always having customers find you within this application. That's how "Google My Business" was launched.

This helped businesses get found on their mapping software. Google my Business (later renamed from its most famous name before called "Google Places") helped anyone with an office or retail location input their information for any type of physical location, Museum, Church, and place of business. All you need is an address, phone number, website, and photos. This kept all of your business information on their mapping application so that customers looking for your business on Google search can see your business information displayed with your address and a phone number, allowing for the opportunity to answer their customers search with more "local relevant information."

This expanded the ability for Google to be able to add information to their mapping software that would have taken them years upon years for Google to do on their own. They had even launched a contributor aspect to Google maps were contributors could identify roads, update building numbers, schools, museums, libraries, and government buildings. They created a hub were everyone made Google maps the authority to find directions for anything.

Imagine the power this had for the first local businesses that decided to add themselves to this application.

Google use to display seven businesses on the maps section of your search, but in 2015 Google changed this only to include three listings at a time per search. This was called the "3 Pack" or how I like to call it the "Rat Pack" (after Sinatra, Dean Martin & Sammy Davis...Still legends). The mover made it more difficult to compete in Google, but this is what we will cover in this book in later chapters. We call this strategy of ranking on Google Maps or any mapping applications like Bing Maps—"Local SEO."

Organic Listings

We have all seen these listings, and they have been there since the dawn of search engines. These listings are ranked by the most relevant to that search query just like Google maps except it is meant for websites where websites rank by relevance and authority. (Learn more about SEO with MOZ and My fave SEO person Rand Fishkin).

Remember when I mentioned "Personal Search"—Google will show web pages that are closest to that person and closest related to that search query in organic listings. So you can literally rank locally with the RAP strategy, and it will help you reach even more traffic.

Chapter 4
The Customer Journey

When I first was given the task to put this into a workable strategy for this company I thought of one major thing to start—I put myself into their customers' shoes.

How could I be part of every phase of a customer's journey to this business model, and what was their intent to want to solve their problem? In what ways did we currently impact and could we impact what a customer's power of decision may be.

Sounds complex but it is easier than you may think.

I thought of my own experience as I had repaired a computer with them before. This experience helped me break down the impact in every aspect of a customer's journey.

Four distinct parts define a customer's path to your business online, and they are; Awareness, Consideration, Intent and finally, Decision.

Let's break down the anatomy of how your business can impact each of these phases to understand how to bring more value to your business to search engine eyes and customers behavior.

Remember "Micro-moments" and consider it on each of the phases below.

My Personal Customer Journey

My Macbook Pro was our home laptop, and it was then four years old. It was such a resourceful device that we used. I was using my laptop for a huge project that was due, All of a sudden it stopped working. My wife was upset, as she had just spent a few hours working on some of her photos beforehand, and now all of the work seemed gone.

I quickly grabbed the computer and tried to fix it. I shut it down a few times, dug into my past IT experience, but to no avail, and it seems like it was its time.

Awareness - I quickly grabbed my phone and started researching the symptoms of the Laptop. And many blogs and forums came up, and I also saw a few videos that claimed "5 min fix" that caught my attention. (This was a way to click bait and did not meet my demand) and from all of my research, I jotted down a set of possible things it could be and what I thought I had to buy in parts to try and fix it myself.

Consideration - All of my parts arrived, and I was ready to get to work, but since the screen was also broken, then I decided to buy the parts for that too. What could go wrong, I have done this before. Well, I failed, as I also came to see the number of other tools I needed to finish what I thought would fix my laptop. So I had to go back to the drawing board, and I kept searching for other ways to fix my device. I then found an older article on Macrumors about this company, and about their expertise in Apple products. I quickly created a new tab on my phone browser and Googled the business name.

Intent - I mainly searched for two keywords at that moment; first, I Googled my repair need plus the device I needed repair. I searched for "Mac book screen repair near me," I had an intention to find some repair shop close to me since my perception of this company at that moment was that it was too far, or may not be close to me. Within that search and to my surprise, I did have one of their retail locations about 3 miles closer than any other competitor, and they were listed on the "map pack." I looked at reviews and saw they had repaired Mac books with success before.

I quickly called for more information to explain my issue. What got me to the door was their offer of "Free Diagnostic," and I called an uber and went to that shop the same day.

Decision - Once in the store, the experience of their shop sold me; quality customer service and my time to "geek" out about my attempt to repair was a great experience. I left a review about my experience, and the cycle began again

Chapter 5
Understand Micro-Moments

Let's break down my experience using Micro-Moments and ways you can implement in your local business. The below layers show the impact of RAP on the Micro-Moments strategy.

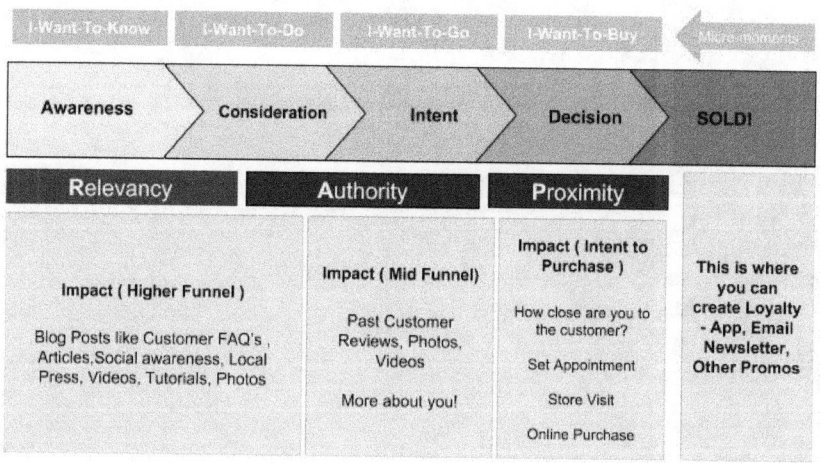

Awareness — "I-Want-to-Know"

I wanted to find a DIY way to repair my Laptop, and I was frustrated because I could not find my answer. Since then other new forums have come up that have better resources, but how come the company I spoke about in earlier chapters was not a resource at that moment (Currently part of our strategy). Imagine the opportunity if I had searched for my issue, found their blog article and saw a local store? This could have saved me grief and be taken straight into the consideration phase.

Consider this for your business, because it is the higher funnel phase and is what I like calling the "Internet Diagnosis" searches like "My phone won't turn on" or "I dropped my phone in the pool." These searches are based on their current experience, because they want to know what to do next but may not be in immediate need. According to Google "51% of Smartphone users have purchased from a company/brand other than the one they intended to because the information provided was "useful."

What do your customers deal with in their daily life that your expert services or products could be the answer?
You need to give them the right "Ideas" that can influence their decision for your services or products?

Example:

You serve an underserved market like "Gluten Free Breakfast." You know there is a need for it, and some customers may have found you via 3rd party sources, but what if you could bring them to your restaurant's website by showing your expertise in having a great gluten-free breakfast.

Write articles like "Fun Sunday Gluten-Free Brunch in Orlando," and show some ideas, and menu items that could make their family Sunday brunch a well deserve event. Or how about impacting questions like "Is Bacon Gluten Free?" You are bringing awareness of your expertise that sets that trust with your customer early on.

Consideration — "I-Want-To-Do"

For us at this company, this is the "I want to repair" moment. I need to repair my screen, I need to replace my battery so how long will it take. What's the cheapest option or the most cost-effective solution, or sometimes based on urgency many customers may just come straight to this consideration phase."

This is where we see searches like.

- "cheap flowers."
- "wedding dress dry cleaners."
- "pest control."
- "Recover hard drive data."
- "emergency plumber

They may still be in the awareness phase but now understand their need a little more clearly. Others may just be in that need at that moment and may not need as much of an awareness phase.

Example:

In the travel segment, this is when they have decided between a resort or hotel room. What is going to offer that traveler the ultimate experience, Roomy space, All-in-one attractions with a lazy river vs. a hotel room that may be closest to their theme park? From the "I-Want-To-Go" phase they have researched and learned from forums, other articles, and Expedia on what they feel would be the best experience. Now it is deciding what would be the most Value, Cost-effective and things to consider based on their initial needs.

Intent - "I-Want-To-Go"

In the marketing world, we call this "Choice Reduction," where the consumer is initially "shopping" for the "their" best solution. In this phase, if you have done a great job at showing your value, it would be up to your website, and stores experience to funnel that customer to contact you. This intent phase is when they have chosen what they need, and Google states that 50% of consumers who conduct a local search on their Smartphone visit a store within a day, and 18% of those searches lead to a purchase within a day.

This is where we see searches like (include "Near Me" "Zip codes" "Regional City Names")

"cheap flowers near me."
"same day wedding dress dry cleaners."
"Pizza near me."
"pest control 32806."
"data recovery near downtown Orlando."
"Miami emergency plumber."

This is where Local SEO is most important, and you want to be found in the Maps for these types of highly relevant searches. People are looking for proximity and convenience, What's closest to them that can meet their needs the quickest.

Decision - "I-Want-To-Buy"

Local SEO is also effective in this phase, and this is where your new customer is already interested but may look at reviews, past experiences that could impact their experience with your brand. This is the touchdown for your local business, and you need to show your value based on this experience.

Consumers will heavily rely on what others say about you to make their decision. This is why you want to be able to give the best experience you can for your customers to succeed. Products and services are also impacted when influencers have taken it in other forms like video. YouTube review videos, Haul videos and "test drives" help when influencers and local customers have added your business as part of their life experiences, and where word-of-mouth used to reign as a stamp of approval, this has taken over.
Make sure to deliver the best experience possible; this is the best rule. Doing this does not cost you much but a smile and a helpful attitude that can bring you these opportunities. As explained above, your customers are aware, and they want to choose what's best for them.

Chapter 6
Now let's roll up our sleeves and get working.

According to a recent article on Local Search Association website (lsainsider.com), a study by BrandMuscle says that almost 56% of local retailers do not have a listing on Google and have not claimed their Google my business profile. WHAT? Really? This is a shame, Why? Because most businesses focus on their operations first or most hire "shady" marketing agencies and freelancers that tend to overcharge or even outright steal a business owners money and not do any meaningful SEO for that local shop.

Tip: *As a business owner, you have to be aware of digital marketing, because this will help in knowing who you are hiring. In my blog, I cover sites that will teach you and keep you updated.*

If you don't have a Google My Business listing, it is the right time to get one. There are a few things to consider before creating a listing. First, you need to make sure you have the correct mailing address, Phone number, and website. These three pieces of information will need to remain consistent through all of the directory listings you will be signing up for.

Your NAP can help with RAP.

Consistency in your business data is called **NAPW**, and this stands for Name, Address, Phone Number and Website and keeping this information consistent will help you with ranking in the desired

3--pack on Google maps and other mapping web applications like Bing Maps.

There are other attributes to NAP that also need to remain consistent, as some directories may ask for the following, Hours of operation, First date of operation, Business email, social media URLs like Facebook, Instagram, YouTube, owners name, services or products, photos, business description, and categories.

Out of all of the above information, there are four we really need to expand on the most, and those are Business descriptions, Categories, and photos.

Your Business Name

I beg of you to please not to engage in changing your business name on Google My Business. Many businesses have started the practice of adding their business name and a keyword and although this tends to do well for a period of time you are still breaking that NAP consistency stated above. You also want to avoid this since Google can track spammy practices and may update their algorithm to filter these types of manipulations in the future.

Back in 2012, Google did an algorithm update that lowered the rankings of websites and business that had little quality, confusing verticals and little to nothing to offer to the internet. These websites included their keyword as the domain name. This was called EMD (Exact Match Domain).

A good example would be if a business that was maybe called Joes Dry Cleaners had a domain with something like "Miamidrycleaners.com" where there might not have been any consideration in working on their brand but just for the means of ranking for the keyword "Miami Dry Cleaners."

Tip: *Stay Legit! Stay clean and do the hard work, as putting in the hard work now will pay off in the future. Don't get so focused on your competitor's rankings if they are doing these types of sketchy practices. Stay away from sites that may promise you the world, and mostly worry about how you can represent your brand and business online to bring value and excellent customer service.*

Categories

Categories need to remain important through this process since you will be asked what category your business falls under. You need to remain specific and analyze what you are adding to categorize your business. Selecting too many categories that are all different will confuse search engines, (Google has well-defined help sections about this which shows how essential this step is for our RAP process). Choosing just the right amount that explains your business is the right way to define categorization on local directories.

Let's look at one example:

A local muffler shop will want to add their main service as their primary category, instead of just "Automotive Repair Shop" this owner should select more specifically what his/her main service includes. This category may be "Muffler Shop." But wait, what if he also services vehicles for Oil changes? Then the 2nd category can include "Oil Change Service." But keep your categories simple, and remember that you're a Muffler shop. Don't add "Transmission Service" just because you would like to have some customers that may want transmission repair. You need to focus on your "Main Business," which may include simple upsells that match your type of business.

Description

Let's create an accurate description of your business. You want to create a narrative that will sell your service or products, and not just add many keywords that you wish to show up for. Make what you offer simple, easy to understand and straight to the point. I suggest to keep it around 200 words max.

Description Part 1

Start off with your location. What significant landmarks are you close to, and are you on a major intersection?

Your first two sentences should be something like the following; (I highlighted the geography specific keywords to add)

Local for local fresh flowers? Our flower shop is located near Washington street between South orange ave and 113th circle, and we are in the same plaza as the Piggly Wiggly supermarket and love serving our Orlando customer base.

Give your potential customer a sense of direction of where you are located. The more famous the landmark, Plaza or Mall, the more you should consider adding it to your description since people may search by landmarks for your product or service.

Description Part 2

"Naturally," consider including some keywords within your description, but you'd still want it to be easy to understand. Some will be tempted to "stuff" keywords within their description, but this is not good for our strategy since Google may see this as spammy. Be careful, because you would want to add your most sought out product or service as a keyword and also include some call to actions (CTAs) that include value propositions.

Let's continue with the flower shop example: (I Have highlighted the most important keywords in this description).

We have a dozen red roses to show your wife or girlfriend how much you love her. Did you make a mistake? At Main Street Flowers we have a variety of carnations and tulips available for pickup or delivery. Our flowers last for two weeks, or they are completely FREE. We include careful handling instructions so that your representation of your emotions can last for quite some time. Online ordering available, Walk-ins always welcome.

Note: When considering the value proposition, there may be ways to add more value to your business with behavioral trigger words that can impact the person's decision-making process. Words that include synonyms for Price, Time, or things that include emotion "inspiring," "Funny," "Brilliant" can show your brand's voice and make your potential customer more interested in your business.

Photos

The experience of your customer is essential to how your customer will do business with you and how they will make a decision on purchasing your product or service. At the company I did work with, one of the biggest things I learned from their creative director was how valuable this process is to the customer acquisition. If you do have a solid interior design for your office or shop, it is because you want to let your customers know what they are going to experience.

We all do it, and we like to make sure that where we eat, play, relax and shop is a safe, clean and an environment that can meet our needs. You are inclined to go to a restaurant that shows a delicious dish rather than a restaurant with no pictures because you "trust" what they are showing will meet your needs.

This is how you should approach your pictures for your business.

Below are the types of pictures you will need before setting up any kind of directory listing.

1. **Exterior photos**: You would want to be able to show the place your location belongs to, and what stores are near you? How your store looks when the customer drives by.

2. **Interior Photos**: Is your location, Fun, and Hip, or is it romantic? Are you a super techie? Showing a location that is clean, interesting and matches your verticals ideal demographic should be displayed on your directories.

3. **Product/Service Photos**: In the case of the flower shop above, you would want to show that photos of the type of arrangements that you have delivered in the past include red roses, tulips, and carnations as added to the description. If you're a service-based

business, include "Action shots" of your employees working on the customer's needs, whether that's fixing a computer or cleaning a carpet, you want to show what you service.

4. **Team Photos**: Showing a happy team can help in increasing that "trust" factor with your potential customers. Make sure to include your employees with branded swag to show your brand and professional culture.

5. **Branded Photos**: These are more standard and require Adding your Logo or branded action photos as your cover or profile picture. If you own a franchise, your franchisor will have this ready for you.

6. **Video & 360 Photos**: Before writing this book, Google recently introduced major assets you could add to your Google my business profile. Those include videos and 360 panoramic photos, both of which can enrich your business details with more complexity about the services or products you offer.

Tip: Do you have a mobile business? Then you can be on Google My Business also. Your photos will be even more critical. Have a food truck? Home services? Take a picture of your wrapped van, or car, your team with branded swag and some equipment to show that you're a trustworthy vendor they can use.

Why such a focus on consistency?

Google needs to legitimize your business and wants to see this consistency in your NAPW. It also wants to understand what verticals you are most relevant for. It needs to make that connection to your industry to understand which search queries other than your business name you are going to be more relevant for. NAP also helps Google and other search engines not only to understand what your information is but your locations and other attributed factors like your photos and reviews.

Tip: If you're a regional or national business with more than one location consider applying for a Google My business and Bing Places Brand account. It takes a while, but you have some time while you gather all of the above info.

Chapter 7
What's R.A.P.?

RAP stands for Relevance, Authority, and Proximity. All three have their own strategy, but all three may also bring value to one another. I felt that introducing the meaning early on could help you understand the breakdown and power of these three factors.

Relevancy: Defined as the content on your website, while attributes like categories, business description tends to also help with this strategy. We will talk about major factors that relate to this and what you will need to do on your website whether you have one location, many or even if you are a franchise.

Authority: How authoritative are you for your vertical or industry? What websites directories mention your company? How many reviews are attributed to your product or service? Google wants to define your business but also needs to see whether you are worthy of their customer's search query.

Proximity: How close your customers may be to your business or your competitors business.

We will be going into each topic deeper in the next few chapters.

Chapter 8
Let's be Relevant

For this first strategy, your business website and user experience are very important, and what you add to your business website will help define the quality Google is looking for from you. Make sure you have a conversation with your web developer or have him read this chapter, as this will accurately define what needs to be done on your website to build towards being relevant to Google.

Before I breakdown relevancy by business types, there are a couple of things you will want to research on, just to ensure you know what will be right for your business.

1. **Don't have a Website**? Consider investing in one. Most small web development agencies can help you create an astounding "original" website. If you have a slim budget, consider using Wordpress. Wordpress is what we call a CMS (Content Management System), which lets you create and deploy a website in a user-friendly format. You can also buy templates that you can add to Wordpress for less than $50 bucks by using sites like Themeforest.net. Themeforest also has services to help you implement their designs for you, so you only have to focus on

content.

Google my business does offer you a free one-page website, You can also buy a domain name via Google my business. This is the last resort but can also be effective. Remember to stay consistent by acquiring a domain that matches your brand and using this on all directories you build.

Tip: Don't be cheap on your website, everyone has a starting point but as you grow your business; invest in yourself. Be original and hire great developers and designers that can help your business thrive. Excellent customer experience also starts with a great website.

2. **Schema Markup**: (aka Rich Snippet) involves adding "Markup" to your site so that search engines can understand data points within your website. With Schema you can tell search engines that you are a "Local Business," and you tell them "Your Address & Phone Number." In some cases, you may even show your type of business. Example, a schema exists that identifies as being a "Lawyer," "Type of Lawyer" and even specific "Branches" of the law firm. To get a full list of what to use to define your business, go to Schema.org (You'd want to implement this on your whole website).

I will start by breaking it down by the type of business:

Small — One shop business

Regional and National business — more than one location

Each has a specific way to define their local business and will have its own strategy for relevancy, but you will still want to read the "small" first since it will likely have some of the intricacies that will also apply to regional chains and other national sites.

When building a website, there are many more SEO factors to consider. They range from title tags, meta description to image alt tags and securing your web address with SSL. I will only be covering the super basic so that you can understand the RAP marketing strategy. For a more in-depth explanation to optimize your website visit: https://moz.com/learn/seo

Small Business:

Most local businesses can benefit considerably from a great local SEO strategy. A local business would have more time to dedicate to making sure their brand, website, content and business information are consistent and are of quality.

Let's start with the homepage. This will be your most important page for your local business. It is where your brand lives and where Google may direct most of the customers you want. There are a couple of elements you need for a successful homepage; as a minimum, you would want the following on your homepage.

1. Your brand and business name

2. Your Street address and your phone number

3. Localized content about your business, just like significant landmarks near you, the name of the mall or plaza, major intersections and streets were your business is located.

4. Your main categories that describe your business and these categories may be "Flower Shop," "Wedding Dress Shop," "Car Mechanic" and also include keywords that identify the specific business and other services you may offer.

5. Pictures of your business - Show your customers' experience and perhaps even include team members or group team photo

Second is your service pages, and the idea is to structure your website by service category, and then break it down by the type of service.

Example:

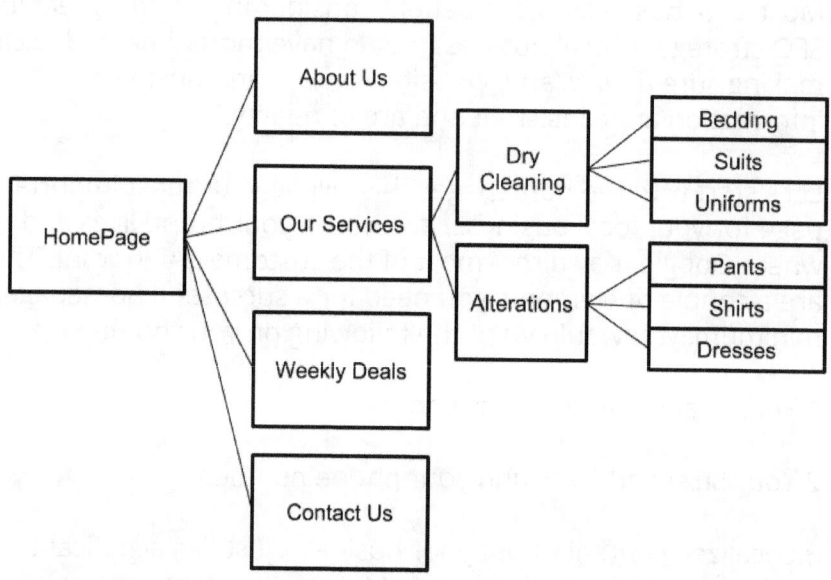

You would want to do this by creating "Content Pages." These are keyword rich pages that help identify the type of services you are offering for your business, and it breaks it down by pages that can easily identify keyword opportunities and also can help determine a specific need for a customer.

For these pages, you want to create content that has both answers for your customers and also can help search engines understand more about your business.

In the mind map above, a dry cleaning service will have a content page that speaks about their Dry cleaning service. This category will talk about their process, type of materials they can dry clean and then link to separate pages that talk about those materials.

The right structured URL will read:
Joesdrycleaning.com/our-services/dry-cleaning/bedding

The bedding page would talk about the type of bedding they dry clean, their process and why bedding should be dry cleaned. Also, including more details like a table with types of bedding and prices can also increase not only the usefulness for the customer but bring even more relevance for search queries like, "Price to dry clean king size bedspread."

Tip: Don't be scared to take it to the next level, If you want to be even better at a website you could also include service comparisons. These tables can identify your price and service versus your competitors.

The key is making the content page useful for your customers while making it relevant for search engines.

Tip: Selling Goods Or Products?
If you sell products like a supermarket or clothing store you can include pages that are more useful to your customers. These pages could consist of, Coupons, Specials, Recipes (Identifying product, product description and isle they can find it at within the recipe content) and an "about us" page that can talk about your specific type of retail product—example is an Organic food store instead of just "supermarket."

The last part of the website additions is implementing schema markup that includes the following to your site. Your developer will know the best way of realizing this.

http://schema.org/LocalBusiness

2. You also want to pick what type of organization your business falls under and the type of local business. Stay consistent and follow the categories you have already chosen for your business in the first chapter.

3. Consider adding a Google Map for the Map Schema

4. Reviews - Correctly adding this schema can help you gain more clicks because it adds your rating, "Physical" stars, to your organic listings.

Let's say you scale your business to more than one location, or you currently have a lot of sites within your region. This is how you should implement your site.

Regional Business

This apparently means you have more than one location, and this strategy is a bit different because you still want to create high-quality content that talks about your business but you want to identify each of your locations separately as well.

See regional and national example below.

Example:

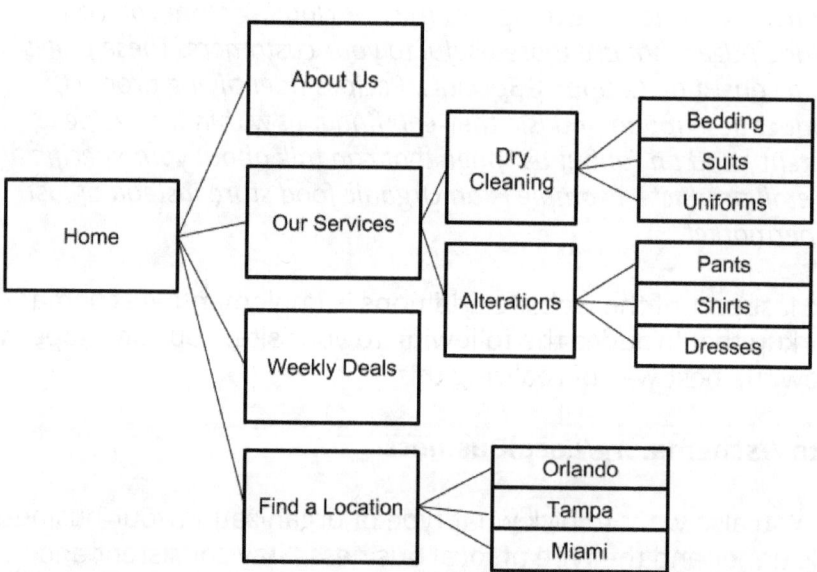

Let's start with the homepage; the home page will differ slightly to a local page because you don't need to add a specific location. In fact, your homepage for a regional or national brand should convey what services you offer, and it should include a call to actions that help customers find their nearest location to direct them to a service funnel to book their needs from your business.

You still want to include content pages just like the small business structure, but in this section, we want to go over building location pages specifically.

There are two ways you can build this, Regional with location specific, or just location specific. Both have their benefit but none is greater than the other, the main difference is ranking for regional terms more often than just city specific terms.

A.) Regional plus city will look like the following structure

bbqgeek.com/Miami/coral-gables

You may have more than one location in Miami, each within a sub-city of Miami.

B.) The city only locations will look like the following structure

bbqgeek.com/coral-gables

Both are correct, but one takes a bit more work to accomplish, and if you have the luxury of a big team with time, then I recommend regional plus city.

Note: Do not create specific pages for keywords that have geographies, an example would be "smithlawyer.com/Orlando-car accident" or "smithlawyer.com/long-island-boat-accidents." These could be considered gateway pages that may not be useful enough for the searcher and may increase your workload with little to no benefit for local SEO.

Let's focus on what you will add to your locations page.

1. **Store name or Store Number** — You want to add an identifier to this specific location, not only brand

2. **Address & Phone** — This is specific to the location you are creating this page for

3. **Google Map** — Add an interactive Google map to this page

(Checkout Google Map API)

4. **Create a section with images from your store** — Going back to customer experience; try and sell the customer on the reason to come in, add exterior and interior photos, product or service and also consider adding team pics.

5. **Location-specific video** — Have a small 15 seconds commercial for your business, and consider adding this content too. It is optional but can help improve the messaging of your brand. Want a Free commercial? Try Onsite Director from Google. It's free if you try their YouTube ads.

6. **Add employees** — Does this location have public facing key employees; how about sales executive and office president? Consider adding these types of employees with a headshot, name, and position, as this brings more personalization to your page.

7. **Content**. Using the same rules as the flower shop in the previous chapters, you could add more info on your business, its locations, nearby landmarks and several keywords within the content. Add subheaders that talk about specific services and give more contexts to your return or warranty policy, along with any other value that can solidify the trust in your business.

8. **(Optional) Add custom forms for each location that can send leads** to that specific location — this is not for SEO but more for capturing these leads. A lot of traffic will be coming to your site from Google maps and adding a form can help you capture leads that will assist that customer with their location.

One more thing before the next chapter.........

Build a Local Business Blog

Lastly, you want to build a blog. But don't just write anything, you need to be creative and include more info about your business. Make your brand discoverable and show what your business stands for and why they should hire you. Blog ideas include team member promotions, latest in-house recipe, even local sponsorships or non-profit events. You want to show you are an active member of the community and that your business is a staple of that community.

This blog should also help attract local attention and create a "Buzz" were other sites can link to you. Some ideas I have given to small businesses are

● Plumbers: Create a heat map or get data about what zip codes or parts of the city gets the most clogged toilets (It should be humorous and get areas to battle each other)

● Another excellent plumbing idea: Write a story about that wedding ring you helped a wife find after ten years.

● Lawyers: List stories "If sensitivity and confidentiality is not a factor" of the craziest accidents or cases clients may call you about (you may title it: Crazy Cases Friday)

● Restaurants: How about naming a menu item after the local high school football quarterback, or having a straight "A" student name a burger. This can also get some local Press.

● "FAQ Tuesdays" Gather your most asked questions whether it is brand specific or a generic question about your industry and answer with the most detailed explanations, along with tables, graphs and other data points that enrich your content.

You may want to make your blog not only enjoyable but to attract local press as well. This creates a segway to our next chapter about building authority.

Chapter 9
Build Authority

Authority establishes and legitimizes your business in any search engine's eyes. Authority is the process of building "mentions" about your business on other sites that may link back to your website and content. In SEO this is called "linked building" and depending on how much authority the website that mentions you have (based on popularity, quality, and other mentions), search engines will award these websites with an authority metric also known as Pagerank.

Carry out more study on (Google about Pagerank and their ranking system, because it is how they started their search engine) other tools like Moz which have named their form of calculated authority as Domain Authority or DA. Where a Domain can have a metric of 1 to 100, where 100 is the most authoritative. Pages can also be ranked this way, and they are called "Page Authority" or PA.

Depending on the DA and the PA of the website that links to your page, it is how you earn your own DA and PA for your site. Higher authority means better rankings and search engines will see you as relevant.

Tip: *Building links to your website or also know as link building is a science in it itself, and concerns the type of links you build to the process of building links that closely relate to your content. Link building is a huge part of SEO, and I suggest reading the book from search engine journal, SEO 101. Great co-authors and content to get you started.... Beware of scammers, Never, ever, ever buy links and if in doubt, ask your peers if a company may be legitimate or not. There are many Subreddits on reddit.com for SEO, and others that you can inbox and twitter that will guide you to the right path.*

When it comes to local SEO, it is a bit different, and you can establish authority with the above example, as it is the primary way to do so. Second is directory listings; what directory websites are listing your business info about your website or store location page? These directories are also called citations, and creating these directories is called citation building.

The major directories you should invest time in building yourself is the following.

1. Google My Business
2. Bing Maps
3. Facebook Local Page
4. Yelp
5. Apple Maps
6. Yahoo Maps

Remember to be consistent as mentioned before; Keep the NAPW the same within these citations.

But those are not the only directories that exist, about 1,000+ directories exist and manually adding your business to the most relevant of those could get exhausting and overwhelming.

There are the top local SEO services I recommend for you to invest in. My favorite is Whitespark & Yext.

Whitespark

WhiteSpark is a Canadian Local SEO service, founded by Darren Shaw in 2010, and this company knows how to clean-up your citations and get you all of the directories that will, in turn, take you to the 3-Pack of directories.

With Whitespark there are two main services that will impact your business.

Citation Audit — This service will help you with auditing and repairing all of the current directories you may be listed in, which may have inconsistencies. These services will include fixing your business name, address, phone number, Web site address, and categories. I highly recommend this service if you have been in business for more than 90 days. Sometimes your business data may get picked up by other directories, and they may not have the most accurate info. Whitespark will make it right.

Citation Building - This is where you will build your authority, and they will manually build a set amount of citations that will impact your business on a local level. One of the critical things of why I like whiteSpark is because they will also build citations on websites that are closely related to your vertical. If you are a restaurant, they will find directory listings of restaurants that would fit your business. As an example, if are the owner of a pizza shop, they will build citations and add your business to directory listings that are related to Italian restaurants, Pizza restaurants, etc. This allows Google to understand your verticals, thus making you more authoritative in your community for "Pizza."

Whitespark has a lot of different packages, so consult with them on what would work best for your business. If you own a mobile business, then they will create a package defined for your business without having to show an address.

Yext

A second great option is Yext. Yext started their business in Nov 2006, and have since exploded in business. Yext is a powerful tool since it works with partners to update and consolidate your information at scale. You only input your information once. Make sure to gather all of the above first.

Yext will deploy your information to all major directories you need to be in and "Suppress" any information that might cause Google to be confused like, the wrong phone number, business name or address.

Centralizing your brand info in one location — Yext is known as a DKM platform (Digital Knowledge Management) as it focuses on centralizing your business information and making sure that the most relevant partners have the same consistent information about your local business, such as business name, categories, pictures. They also offer a lot of other tools to help you with tracking reviews and other information on your brand and even adding elements to your website that helps Google understand your site.

Bright local

Bright local is another excellent local SEO company that mixes both the automation of aggregating your business information and manually adding your business information to directories.

Their citation burst package is only 50 bucks and adds you to the 3 top aggregators of business information, which are Axiom, Express Update & Factual. They charge about $1 - $2 per directory listing they build for you. It's a much cheaper option and has a lot more customized opportunities. If you have a lower budget, you can stretch out your strategy by purchasing a citation burst the first month and investing 50 bucks a month in manual submissions. It's a great solution to build your local citations little by little.

Moz Local

As mentioned earlier on in this book, Moz is one of my favorite websites for SEO fundamentals and SEO tools. They came out with a Local SEO product similar to Yext and Bright Local with packages starting at $99. Although they don't suppress bad info, they do Submit to Axiom, Express Update and Factual, and lets you know what other directories may have duplicates of your business information. They may expand to have a lot more features, but at the time of writing this, I feel like they have some ways to go to challenge the big guys like Yext and Whitespark.

Do it Yourself

Although this will take quite a bit of time, I don't advise it if you have multiple business listings, unless you have a large staff and each is dedicated to one of your listings. There are a few ways to do this;

New Listing — If you're doing this for a new location, Start With Google My Business, Bing Maps, Yelp, & Apple Maps as mentioned before. You can submit to Axiom, Express Update and Factual yourself, but to speed things up, I recommend creating an account with Bright Local and paying them $50 to do the citation burst package. This will speed some things up for you if you don't want to go through all of the verifications.

Older Business Listings — Been in Business for a while? Audit and clean up your listings, and the best way to do this is to Google your business phone number. This will bring up a lot of sites that contain your number and within these results will be citations. It's a long process, but with patience, you could gather the sites you are listed on. Be detailed and keep a running spreadsheet with all of these sites. Once the list is complete go one by one and claim your listing to verify your information. Remember to keep a consistency in your business information, same name, phone number, address, & website.

Time to build — This step is time-consuming but not hard. This step must be done after you have audited your directory listings and cleaned up any bad information. This is your second step if you are a new listing.
The first thing you're going to do is create a new spreadsheet, (have your photos, videos, and business information ready) then you will create a spreadsheet to keep track of directories.
In this spreadsheet you will add a tab for each competitor that you see appears when doing your keyword search.

Now we will engage in Keyword research. If you own a plumbing business, you will want to search for "plumber + city" and create a tab on your spreadsheet for each of the three competitors that appear. Try to search for more than one keyword. Try Keywords like "plumbers near me," "cheap plumbers," "plumbers nearby," "plumbers + zip code," etc. Record their business name and phone number on the spreadsheet. Once you have added the competitors to the spreadsheet, start with your first competitor, by Googling his name and phone number. This will bring up directory listings they are listed on. You will want to copy the URLs of the listings you are currently NOT in. This helps you find directories that are either industry or geography specific. Also, it helps you see what directories your competitors used to rank for that specific keyword or phrase allowing you to find directory listings that Google saw as authoritative. Lastly, make sure your category matches for all of the listings you are working on.

Adding Information — This step is crucial as many people may be tempted to copy and paste their business info and not fill out the directory listings completely. I advise you to fill out every little detail — from the year you started your business to employee headshots and bios. Furthermore, you may add a well-written description of your business, services or products and photos that you have already used for Google My Business. Make sure to add title and captions to the photos that describe the pictures and are keyword rich.

Join the BBB, Regional & Local Chamber of commerce— This will cost you some money, but it proves to be effective in creating authority with Google since its exclusiveness sits behind a paid membership and shows "trust." If not all three, at the least join your local Chamber of commerce and make sure you treat that listing exactly how you would manage all of the other listings you just created. Include keywords, descriptions, photos, and fill out every bit of information it asks for. I will cover more about this in the next chapter.

The more you wait, the longer it would take to rank on Google Maps, and I suggest creating a strategy every day to start working on your plan because it will help you explode your business to the next level locally.

Chapter 10
The System is defined by proximity & Trust

One of the most critical parts of the algorithm to ranking for those profitable keyword searches is proximity. Google has expanded their ranking algorithm to help consumers find what's closest to them, regardless of how much optimization you have done to your business. This is great for the consumer and it is one of the phases we have the least control on. If you search and you are at your house, school, church and your competitor is closer to these locations than your business; it means they may show up higher in rankings than your location.

In my opinion, Google does this to help their revenue with their Adwords platform. It makes sense to make it helpful for the consumer, but you can still win these positions with an Ad on Google Maps, in which, it is activated when you add your Google My business location to your Adwords account; also called location extension—(an extension of your ad that displays your business information and hours by using your Google My Business profile).

When you invest time into becoming more relevant than your competitors, Google will rank your business higher even if you were further back prior to. There are still some things that can be done in this phase that apply to both relevance and proximity. Doing those things will surely cost you some money, but what you are looking to do here is to establish your business within your community. Not only embedding yourself and showing Google that you're a legitimate business within that community but that you're relevant to the products or services you offer. You are going to want to do the following.

1. **Join your local chamber of commerce** — Find your local chamber of commerce and become a member of the package that includes the website directory, and it will establish your local authority with Google. You want Google to legitimize your business within your region, and this is the best way of telling Google how to do it. Make sure you complete every single question, Add relevant keywords, photos, and make your own custom business description for this directory

2. **Better Business Bureau®** — The BBB builds trust, and also is superb for building your "trust Flow." It is a very exclusive list of business, which Google considers when legitimizing your business within your community. I know about the yearly cost, but you are investing in trust, and not just SEO. Remember, trust is what matters.

3. **Non-Profit Sponsorships** — You obviously want to look for what your business is most passionate about, and it could range from animal shelters to local arts. They all have websites, so see what business partnerships could help in creating a link to your website.

4. **Local Event Sponsorships** — Is there a Christmas parade, Local school football team, and how about a monthly farmers market? All of these events have two things in common —they have a website that your business can be part of, and they also bring a lot of positive press, which, in turn, creates more local relevance that people can link back to your business website.

5. **School Discounts** — Universities and private schools offer a student page that lists local businesses, which offer discounts to their students. Find your local schools and see if they have such page, and offer a discount that is meaningful to their students and creates exclusivity. I suggest 10% and higher as this can help get traffic into your local business. This strategy will create the

opportunity to show your business name, address, phone and website that creates a strong authority in Google's eyes. Finding these opportunities is simple, just do a Google search with the school's name and include "Local Discount" within the search. If it is hard to find the page, contact the school, then speak to the student government, student affairs department and get more information from them.

Building authority in Google's eyes is a crucial aspect to the Local SEO strategy and requires being actively engaged as part of your community by taking part in non-profit volunteering to joining causes that your business stands for. It will help in gaining PR opportunities and connections to local bloggers that can be linked back to your website. For a more comprehensive SEO strategy that is not only focused on Local SEO, you can concentrate on what we call Link-Building, which also helps build authority for your business. There are many options for this as mentioned before.

Some Link Building opportunities may be spam, and some are real opportunities, thus ensure you educate yourself on what's ethical in SEO so that you and your brand do not suffer if Google changes their ranking algorithms to filter out spams. This may cause your website to go under penalty, and you may be "De-Indexed" from Google. I recommend looking up the "Marketing Flywheel" method by Rand Fishkin to create an effective link building campaign that will help your business succeed in "trust" and SEO.

Chapter 11
Let's Review Your Business

Reviews are one of the most critical factors that will bring you success. When looking for a restaurant or any other store, we look for their reviews —we have all done it before. Reviews are a transparent peer-to-peer way to see how the business can meet the consumers need or experience. In fact, this "trust" factor can be attributed to higher rates of conversion.

According to Brightlocal, in 2014, "88% of consumers say they trust online reviews as much as personal recommendations." And that's not all, positive reviews are also helpful with visibility, and according to Google "High-quality, positive reviews from your customers will improve your business's visibility." Companies like Yelp have built their business around this concept, and it has made Yelp very successful in building a large network of businesses and users alike. Your business gets reviews whether you want them or not, and almost all online directories have a "review this business" aspect to their website. As a marketer and business owner, you need to take care of your reputation.

Improve Your Customer Service

If you want to make an impact in reviews, the simple fact of improving your overall customer service will make an organic impression with your customers, and going the extra mile will excite them to take that extra step of becoming a brand advocate. According to a recent study by The Consumer Barometer Survey and Google, in 2015, "14% of Brand Advocates post a review online, compared to just 8% of non-Brand Advocates."

Taking the step into optimizing your customer's experience will have that online impact that will create a holistic ability to gain reviews about your business. Other things that may impact these reviews are simple things like how clean was your shop? How presentable and professionally did you and your staff looks? How easy was the sales process? Is your website easy to navigate and find information? You want to optimize anything that creates a better customer experience and can improve how your customer may view your business.

The quality of your product or service matters

I have read many reviews, while some are neutral, I see positives all of the time, but the one major review type I see more often is negative reviews. The majority of these reviews are all based on the quality of the product or service. Make sure your product or service is not only useful but meets the higher demand of the consumer.

As an example, in the company I worked for, we offer the best electronics parts from reputable suppliers which makes our service more expensive than the competitors, but the rate of customers coming back for issues is way lower than any of our competition. Improve your product or service to what you would expect as a consumer. If you empathize with their needs and use your knowledge to help them, then this will create a positive experience worthy of a positive review.

Fake reviews happen, respond and report

My email box gets slammed with questions on how to resolve fake reviews. Understand that there is a clear difference between fake and unfair. Unfair online reviews are something that you will have to work directly with that customer. With fake reviews, you could feel hopeless, because all of your hard work on the quality of your business seems to go down the drain, and there is no hope.

In fact, there are some things you can do to remove these. You will first have to identify whether it is a fake review. There are two basics to a fake reviewer. First, they would only have one review for a business. Usually, these types of accounts are created to demote a business and are purchased through online "gigs" that many horrible competitors practice in order to gain more visibility for themselves.

To identify this, you will simply have to click on the name of the reviewer, and you will see all of the reviews they have left before yours. If they have left only yours, then your probability of getting it removed increases considerably. Alternatively, there is a second approach to this. Does this user only leave bad reviews to other businesses like yours? If so they could be using the same account to leave bad reviews for all of the surrounding business; thus, with a simple analysis, you can tell what local business is doing this shady practice.

Once you have analyzed the review follow these steps:

First, you want to positively respond to the review, by shedding light on what the expected outcome should have been and what you're willing to do next. 90% of the time you won't get a reply, but while you are marking this review for deletion, you are showing other potential customers that you care.

Second, you will want to flag the review. This process is super simple. Flagging the review is basically clicking on the flag icon usually on the top right of the review. This process alerts Google or any other directory of the comment and "flags" it in their system. Don't do this often, and one time will do.

Third, you can directly report it to Google or the directory listing you are working with. With Google, there are three great ways to do this. The first option is to call a Google my business specialist, and this is easy if you are already a paying Adwords customer since you have the ability to call them directly if you are having issues with Adwords. After calling **1-866-2GOOGLE**, you will have to give them your Adwords CID located in the top right-hand corner, and before the call ends, ask them to please email you as this will contain the contact info of their person you are speaking with.

The second option is to post on their forum at en.advertisercommunity.com, this option is slower but can give you an opportunity to connect directly with their core team. Create a concise post with screenshots and wait for their responses.

The last one that has worked for me is to use Twitter. To start, you will want to follow @GoogleMyBiz on Twitter. Second, send a tweet about your business and a link to the fake review. Usually, they will DM you for more information.

Don't take reviews for granted

Start to respond to reviews, talk to your customers and thank them for their business, One major study by ReviewTrackers found that "53.3% percent of customers expect businesses to respond to their online review within seven days." If you don't have the time to do it, assign a manager that can help you respond, then look out for things like grammar, spellings, and how you react to a negative review. The wrong response can also cause the worst reaction than just dealing with a bad review. Many online platforms exist to help you track and control the reviews you're getting online, and two major platforms that are winning in this space are Yext and Reviewtrackers. Keep on top of your reviews, and you will reap the benefits.

Don't buy fake reviews

Positive or negative reviews can be purchased directly or indirectly. Don't do it, and If a website or vendor is guaranteeing you a number of reviews, it is too good to be true, don't fall for it. I have seen many times were a local business, or a franchise owner has invested dollars into buying reviews, only to end up six months later were they first started.

Google uses its own detection algorithms that can sniff fake reviews, and when caught it will automatically remove them. This may have an impact on your visibility in the short term, but it may also create a negative influence on Google's trust in your business. In Yelp, for example, they may even delete, remove or freeze your business and not allow you to show up as often. Lastly, do not incentivize customers for reviews as it is against Google policy. You will want to create reviews naturally, although it may seem too long everything in SEO takes time, if it did not, it would be too easy to "Game" the system.

Try to gain a review at the transaction level. Simple ways to do this is to have your staff say the following: "If you had a great experience, please review us on Google." Other methods that I have seen this is if the email address is gathered at the transaction point, then you can email your customers for a review or hand them a flyer on how to find and rate you on Google.

The most creative and empathic way I have seen gained reviews is with an experience I had at a local here in Orlando. My wife Kristy and I had gone to an amazing steakhouse for our anniversary. A few weeks after, I received a "handwritten" postcard thanking me for celebrating my anniversary at their establishment, and at the end of the letter it gave me a website that had links to their review sites, but it was not just a stuffed "review us" postcard. It said, "We would love your feedback to improve our quality of service if you don't mind to take a couple of seconds and go to www. And let us know what you think about our restaurant." This meant a lot more to me and motivated me to "want" to review them. This is how you create a brand advocate without having to "buy" your reviews.

Chapter 12
How to manage more than one location

A lot of my experience in managing multi-location strategies came from my current client work. Through this process, I learned a lot of the basics of how to make sure that your business information is consistent. If you have not yet consolidated all of your locations into one corporate account, you need to start now as a first step. A lot of these directory companies and organizations will allow you to create a "brand" account with a more straightforward process of verifying your business. Register your chain on the top directories to at least keep control of the most important directories.

Major Pain points

There are some major pain points that you need to make sure you are taking control of. Managing user access is vital since managers assigned to profiles can make changes that can impact these listings. Things I have seen before start with name changes to categories and even hours if not done correctly can ruin any hard work in keeping a consistent NAP. Make sure you set standards and rules before giving access. With franchisees and small business owners, I warn them of the possible effects and grant access only to owners and managers. It keeps everything consistent and will allow for more control over your brand profiles.

The second major pain point is keeping directories together in one dashboard. Yext is a great tool for this, but you may run into a higher cost per year. Other than Yext, my trick is to keep a "smartsheet," or Google drive spreadsheet with each corporate store and develop a map of all of the current listings you can find. This will allow you not only to know your local search landscape but also organizes the listings so that you can assign a team member to help you fix it.

Lastly keep a template of your description, the breakdown of your services and logo. Things you may use more than once can be templatized to allow you to become more effective in working with more than one location.

Partner up

One of my favorite things to do is to find potential partners that could work with me. There are plenty of directory listing websites out there that can use your data. Partner up with them by sending them an email, Tweet, Facebook message or using their contact form. Ask if they have a way to bulk upload your locations and become their data source. This method works best with a large number of locations, just remember to have a spreadsheet ready when they respond.

Chapter 13
Social Features

Google My Business has made new social integrations to their platforms to help you reach your customers in different ways. The following are some features you should invest some time in that will help you communicate with your customers using your Google My Business profile. You can add Google posts, add videos, answer direct customer questions and even create an opportunity for texting.

Google Posts

Do you sometimes wish you had the ability to create opportunities to communicate with your customers about your events, local offers, and other educational posts? You can with Google Posts. Google created this in lieu of the connection Google My business had to Google plus before. Posts only last for three days at a time so you will have to commit to weekly posts. The idea is not to overwhelm you but to have an opportunity to show more about the company, and what it offers or even believes in.

Videos

You have the ability to add videos in two ways; as Google Post updates and also to show more of your product or service. Videos are a great way to interact with your customers and even show off your product or service. An excellent way to do this is to gather your frequently asked questions and create a video series that can build that trust with your customer. It also has the benefit of helping you establish a relationship with the consumer before they even interact with your business. Another great potential is to add customer review videos; however, don't buy them, and ensure you create reviews that are genuine.

Q&A

Consumers can now ask local shops questions about their products or services, and they can also respond to your business if they know the answer. This is called the Q&A, and it is located when you Google your business. It is slightly tucked away before the reviews and can be forgotten. There are pros and cons to this feature. The pros are the ability to answer the customer's direct questions that can be read and seen by others; while the con is that any negative feedback you might receive may crawl up in there and if not answered immediately may get worse. Try to stay on top of this as it is something that can be used for good. If you download the Google My Business app, Google will alert you when someone has a question, and Google also does this to the millions of contributors that have reviewed your business.

Texting

Not a social feature, but a great feature to acquire leads that may need a price or a quick question about the services you offer. Set up is simple if you have an extra phone to give room for this. If you don't have a phone, you could also use Google Allo, by simply registering the application with the number you use for your Google profile, and you could use the Google Allo app on your cell phone or desktop. Just remember to be responsive and do not ask for personal information like credit cards or social security numbers. Don't open that can of worms to avoid any legal issues.

Resources

No matter the circumstance, as a business owner you have already taken risks way more complicated than SEO. You now have the power to do this yourself and succeed, don't be suckered into contracts with agencies that may never get you where you want to be.

If you want to learn more or want to enjoy a lot more resources visit my blog jongeek.com and signup for our email list or notifications and keep up to date with our blog. I try to keep the blog as fresh as possible. Other places to consider to help you stay informed are;

Searchengineland.com
searchenginejournal.com
searchenginewatch.com
moz.com/blog
webmasterworld.com

Enjoy and if you have any questions add me on Linkedin and let's connect.

Please share this book with other local businesses, The goal of this book is to help business owners grow their local business and grow their profits to invest back into growing the local American economy.